Hope from the Pure Land Way
in Unnerving Times

Hope from the Pure Land Way in Unnerving Times

John Del Bagno

Pure Land Arts ■ San Francisco ■ 2021

◯
———

Hope from the Pure Land Way in Unnerving Times
by John Del Bagno

Published by Pure Land Arts
PO box 2523
Brisbane, California 94005
purelandartwork.com

ISBN: 978-1-7376973-0-5 trade paperback

Design and composition: www.dmargulis.com

First printing

MANUFACTURED IN THE UNITED STATES OF AMERICA

＿＿＿◯＿＿＿

In Gratitude to Hōnen

O
_____

Contents

○

○
___

Illustrations

○
——

○
___

Some of the Ways to Say Amitābha's Name: The Buddha-name

Namo Amitābha Buddha (India)
Om Amideva Hri (India)
Namo Amituofo (China)
Nam-mô A-di-đà Phật (Vietnam)
Namu Amidabutsu (Japan)

◯
_____

Preface

Work on this book began in the first week of April 2020, as the initial wave of the COVID-19 pandemic took hold in the United States. I continued in my job at a retirement community in California as an essential worker. In my poetry and art life, I had been putting together several works in which I was exploring what the Pure Land Way has to offer to those young people living a life of addiction and hardship. With the arrival of the pandemic, it felt as if we had tipped over into strange and unsure times. This prompted me to expand the scope of the work for a broader audience in a time of widespread anxiety. Some material from the initial project has been rolled over into this book, most notably the print "She will go to the Pure Land" and the poems "We Are Here Afloat" and "Amitābha Is Not Afraid of Me." I encourage you to look to the glossary in the back of the book for definitions of any terms with which you are unfamiliar. Some of the prints in this book are associated with the poems next to which they are printed, but most are not. The poems are all written to be read aloud, each line a spoken phrase.

JDB
August 2021

○
───

Hope from the Pure Land Way in Unnerving Times

Help from Amitābha

○

Introduction

Hōnen (1133–1212 CE) lived in a time of great upheaval for Japanese society. Their world shook with uncertainty as one tragedy after another came upon them: great urban fires, floods, epidemics. The common people lived under the threat of bandits, warring factions, invaders from across the sea and brutal treatment from the Samurai. The government was in disarray as it underwent the transition toward the Shogunate.

Amongst a people full of anxiety, Hōnen sought a way out through the enlightenment that ends suffering. He felt that there must be a teaching of Shakyamuni Buddha that will rescue one, such as he, who cannot follow Shakyamuni's example of renunciation and meditation. While the path of meditation does lead to enlightenment, there are but few today who have the discipline and stamina to reach enlightenment under their own power. Hōnen sought a path that was accessible to the average person caught up in this demanding world. He became certain that the Pure Land Way, with its devotion to Amitābha Buddha, was the path to freedom from suffering.

Amitābha is the Buddha of Infinite Light who loves us exactly as we are and wants to shepherd us toward our enlightenment. Anyone can perform the practice of reciting Amitābha's name. Just by saying the Buddha-name we establish a relationship with Amitābha who has vowed to come at our moment of death and lead us back to his Pure Land, a place of great spiritual power he created through eons of spiritual discipline. In that place there is no pain and one

○
_____

experiences the intense bliss of the higher states of consciousness. It is far easier to make spiritual progress there than it is here in this human world. So much so, that within only one lifetime spent there, enlightenment is reached and we become a Buddha. As a Buddha, we will possess the powers necessary to free other beings from their worlds of suffering. In this way, the purpose of the Pure Land Way is fulfilled.

Inspired by a commentary by Shandao (613–618 CE) on the Pure Land sutras, Hōnen realized that one must drop all other spiritual practices and, as Shandao said, "Think solely upon Amitābha's name, whether walking or standing, sitting or lying down, for a short or long period of time. This is an act which ensures birth in the Pure Land."

Hōnen felt that saying Amitābha's name regularly was the spiritual practice best suited to those living through such unsettled times. Reciting the Buddha-name can be done anywhere in any situation. We can say it out loud, just under our breath or silently to ourselves in our minds. We can sing it in fine harmonies or grumble it out the side of our mouth as we get out of bed to face the day. Kneeling before an altar or sitting on a toilet are both good places to say the Buddha-name as nothing can stain or pollute Amitābha's light.

By saying Amitābha's name in little batches throughout our day, and with our hearts set on being born in the Pure Land, we are doing all the spiritual practice we need to do. Now Amitābha takes over, drawing us toward the Pure Land. Amitābha comes to know us in a very direct way and protects us. However, until death, we will still experience our own bad karma at work in our lives.

○
———

Karma is the cause and effect principle by which we plant good or bad karmic seeds in our consciousness with our deeds and intentions. Then, in the same way in which seeds sprout in the right conditions, so our good and bad karma takes effect in our life when the conditions are right. This impact may be felt in this life or not ripen until one of our future lives. This is why bad things that happen can seem to come out of nowhere.

Who we have been in previous lives continues to affect who we are right now. Who we are now and the actions we are taking are making a deep impression on the person we will become in our next life. We are more a process than a distinct individual. By repeating our evils we cause pain to ourselves in the lives that follow.

The movement from this life to the next can be likened to lighting one candle from another. The two flames are not the same flame, but they are also not two completely different flames. So it is with the person we will be in our next life. We will be a different person, we will look different and maybe speak with a different accent or in another language, but we will also be the same in what drives us, what attracts us and repulses us. There is every likelihood that, left unchecked, our old bad habits will intensify and continue to drive us into ever darker nights of anguish.

Being born into the Pure Land after one's death offers a way to avoid that suffering. The Pure Land actually exists, but it is a different order of being from our experience of this world, in the same way that a dream feels different from our waking life. It is a realm of existence much more refined than our world and so lovely that it makes the human realm look plain and rough. The people all have a golden

_____O_____

radiance as they move steadily forward in their spiritual progress toward enlightenment. The breeze whispers the deepest truths into one's ear, and the birds express the Buddha's teaching in song. One arrives there, born in a blooming lotus, to great fanfare and welcome. After shuttling from life to life, alone for incalculable eons, the Pure Land is a welcome place of respite and community for us.

The Pure Land is also a place of revelation as we are introduced to the truths of existence and are shown ways to unwind the tangled barbed wire of our emotional confusion. We become unburdened and light.

We do not have to be special to follow the Pure Land Way. Following the Pure Land Way does not make us special. In fact, we come to see ever more deeply the foolish state of our minds and our hearts. We can be honest with ourselves and be humbled by our faults, for each slip, error or crime shows us how utterly unequipped we are to attain enlightenment on our own. If we can't do it for ourselves, our only hope is to rely on Amitābha to help us gain enlightenment.

Saying the Buddha-name is an expression of self-love, for we accept ourselves as foolish beings living in a state of confusion. Yet we are loved by Amitābha so there is no need to be self-critical and hateful about it. Instead, we can live in an understanding of ourselves, knowing that Amitābha sees us as worthy of love.

Some, today, find it easier to relate to the Pure Land as a metaphor or as merely a symbol. What is important is to recite the Buddha-name regularly and place one's heart-yearnings on Amitābha. Then birth in the Pure Land is assured.

○
_____

While life in this world holds beauty and love, it is, overall, a world of endurance. We must bear boredoms, little conflicts, and tragedies. Old age, sickness, and death are the hard truths of human life, and they are to be experienced again and again with each new life we live.

A natural part of yearning for the Pure Land is a level of revulsion for this world and its painful ways. The truth that everything is impermanent shows us that we are part of some great churning of events and existences. We exist but briefly, flickering in and out of human lives. We are seeking, always seeking, some static satisfaction, but we can never get hold of it. This frustrates us so much that we indulge in petty vices to distract us from the fragility of life and the pains of our predicament. Sadly, there is no assuaging all of the many losses in a life. We must escape the whole terrible process of human rebirth to be truly free of suffering. We must become enlightened. Thankfully, the Pure Land lies open to us and, once there, our enlightenment will naturally unfold.

Pilgrim at Night

○
─────

The Syllables Flow Out Gently

In the cool evening tonight, resting,
On my back deck with a cup of tea.
A rising star looks solitary to me,
Yet I know that the sharp view of astronomers
Has revealed it to be a vast cluster
Of stars and planets.

When Shakyamuni's wisdom eye opened,
He saw the limitless Buddhas
Spread across world system after world system.
So the star light that reaches me this night
Includes the radiance of a host of Buddhas,
Enough to bathe my tumultuous heart and my cup of tea.

Of all of them, it is Amitābha Buddha whose name I whisper
Over and over into the night.
Each recitation comes lightly
With relaxation of one who has just taken a seat
On a ferry almost missed.
The syllables, they flow out gently,
In the rhythm of small waves
Lapping against a hull.
I am carried along toward the Pure Land
Tonight, on my back deck.

Reciting at Bus Stop

○
_____

Little Fly Going This Way and That

Oops! Little One, you don't want to be in here.
Now, out the window, out this way.
No, no, out here!
C'mon! C'mon!
Oh, what am I going to do with you?
Well, the window is open whenever you are ready.

Amitābha must look at the spinnings
Of my heart-mind in much the same way.

○
———

The Pure Land Way, in Brief

Birth, old age, sickness and death.
Repeat.

Or recite
Amitābha's name
To enter the Pure Land
And become a Buddha.

○
———

Not of the Physical Realm

Whether in dreams or high fever horrors,
We all experience other states of being.
The Pure Land is not of the physical realm.
Just as this Waking Life is one state of being
And the Dream State quite different from it,
So the Pure Land is another state of being:
A realm of bliss, a place of spirit and light,
One created by a Great Buddha,
With his vast loving heart.

A Progression of Pure Land Beliefs

- The historical person, Gautama Shakyamuni, attained a state of being he called enlightenment. He described it as the cessation of suffering.
- All human beings have the potential for enlightenment.
- I can attain enlightenment and have my suffering end.
- Enlightenment can be attained by following Shakyamuni's example of meditation, ethics and wisdom (study).
- I am honest with myself. I do not have the strength to make the effort needed to match Shakyamuni's.
- Shakyamuni also told us about Amitābha Buddha and his vows to rescue us from this world full of pains and fleeting experiences.
- By reciting Amitābha's name regularly throughout my day, I form a relationship with Amitābha.
- I place my heart on rebirth into Amitābha's Pure Land.
- I allow myself to be rescued through Amitābha's love for me, not by my own efforts.
- When I die, Amitābha will be there to take me to the Pure Land.
- All beings in the Pure Land progress quickly to enlightenment.
- As a Buddha, I can free countless other beings.

Two Figures in Pure Land

○
___

As I Age

As I age
I become Old Tree
Rooted to the earth
Through dharma wheels
On the flats of my feet.
The long, sinewy tendrils
Of my roots squirm out through the dirt
In every direction.

Years on,
Deep down, way down,
I reach a depth where the tips of my roots
Can just touch earth wisdom.

I see that
The syrupy flow of life
Moves through my veins
As an ever-present blessing.
Sentience,
Consciousness,
Coming back around to look at itself.

Ah, but I am set upon by thunder blast
After thunder blast.
My bark gets harder,

O
———

The outer layer has formed into long shield shapes.
I've got thick branches, firm,
But going brittle.
Storm, damage
Wind, snap
Deep cracks
Hobble some of my limbs.

Yet Old Tree keeps waiting.
Waiting for the seed of another life to drop,
But this next seed, it will land in the Pure Land,
To germinate and become all golden, of light itself.

Oh, the kindness in Amitābha's realm!
The fussing and fighting here of human society
Unthinkable in the Pure Land!
There is no grasping, no hatred,
And even ignorance is quickly blooming into insight.

So Old Tree stands,
A process, a momentum of life come to fruition
And fading away.
And a day
Will come
When I will be all tumbled down.
But until then, I will wear my years with pride
And someday trade them for a place in Amitābha's Pure Land.

The Veil Between Reciter and Pure Land

○

Only One Main Practice in the Pure Land Way

While there are many effective spiritual practices in Buddhism, in
the Pure Land Way the primary practice is the saying of Amitābha's
name. It is our way of directly engaging with Amitābha, for he imbued
his very name with a spiritual power so that he becomes aware of
each person who recites it.

Saying the Buddha-name is an act of putting our trust in Amitābha,
we go for refuge to him. We have chosen to rely on him as a power
beyond ourselves (other power) to stop our suffering once and for all.
We believe in Amitābha's vows to rescue us from these distressing
human lives.

Reciting Amitābha's name acknowledges that our heart is on its
way to find transcendence of our human aches through rebirth in the
Pure Land. The types of pain we are experiencing now will not last
and cannot stop us from going to the Pure Land.

We are a momentum of consciousness at flow, life to life, in this
insignificant part of the cosmos. Yet, we can place our heart on
something besides ourselves, something beyond ourselves. We can
place our heart on Amitābha.

The habit of reciting Amitābha's name is our ticket to the Pure
Land. What need is there for another spiritual practice when this one
brings us a direct connection to Amitābha? Such a profound contact
coming to us, linking us up with a Great Buddha, how ridiculously
fortunate we are!

○
_____

Amitābha's Vow

I climbed as high as I could
On the rope of meditation,
But my efforts frayed
And all my hopes for
Enlightenment fell down.

I trust now in Amitābha's vow.
It is a rescue cable looped around me,
Drawing me upward.

The way to the Pure Land has opened.
Enlightenment is again in my future.

Dandelion Seed

○
_____

Amitābha's Karma Carries Me

I have released into the wind of Amitābha's pure karma.
It carries me along, a dandelion seed parachute
Caught up on the breeze.
There is no more for me to do.
I float, I wait, knowing that when the seed
Touches the earth, life will remake itself;
Knowing that when I get to the Pure Land
My consciousness will make the great shift,
And all that was I,
Will be enlightenment.

○
_____

What to Call Him

For those new to the Pure Land Way or those who are not affiliated with any one of the existing Pure Land traditions, there is the question of which version of Amitābha's name to recite. Om Amideva Hri? Namo Amidabutsu? Nam-mô A-di-đà Phật? Ultimately, it does not matter. All versions are heard by Amitābha. There are many recordings online to listen to, so see which ones catch your ear and move your heart. When listening to them, remember, you do not have to sing the Buddha-name, just saying it is enough. You can also say it syllable by syllable: A Mi Ta Bha Bud Dha. This allows for a lot of play in saying Amitābha's name, for example, to the different rhythms of whatever song to which we happen to be listening. Like our music, the Buddha-name is a commonplace item in our lives in that it is to be sung or said on an everyday basis. Amitābha's name does not stay on our shrine or altar, it goes with us step by step into all that life brings.

It can be quite nice to chant the Buddha-name in one language after another in solidarity with all of the other reciters around the globe. In whatever way we recite Amitābha's name, it is our bond with Amitābha, who has vowed to pull us through this troublesome life and to welcome us into his Pure Land.

O
———

Ahh, to Finally Rest

Weary of the endless endurance
Of dissatisfaction and disputes,
I will plunk myself down
On my lotus in the Pure Land when I pass away.

After countless human escapades
I will find myself unbound by the ego,
Washed free of habitual karma
And in the joyful company
Of the sangha of the Pure Land.
How good it will be
To share stories of survival
From a life lived
In the desperate human realm.

Together,
We will sit in the Pure Land
As victors,
As survivors
Of a plague of selfishness
Cured only by the burning moxa stick
Of Amitābha's compassionate eye.

Amitābha (with Halo Beings)

○
_____

Getting Started in Reciting Amitābha's Name

Many of us are unfamiliar with the languages in which we can recite the Buddha-name. Don't let this discourage you as you begin. Amitābha knows you mean him when you are saying his name no matter how you pronounce it.

It can be a beautiful habit to recite the Buddha-name in front of a little shrine in one's home, but really, we can say it anywhere in any situation. Whether said aloud, whispered under the breath, or thought in the mind, all are equally spiritually effective in establishing and maintaining our relationship with Amitābha. Over time, our mind will naturally and habitually come back to reciting the Buddha-name.

We do not need to be in a positive frame of mind when we recite; we should let the light of the Buddha-name permeate into all of the dusty parts of our being, our sadnesses, our depressions. Amitābha is an old friend who is there to support us.

Our ingrained negative thought patterns push us around and cause us pain; we can meet them with the Buddha-name. Since we can only think one thought at a time, yet flit between thoughts at incredible speeds, we can crowd out haunting thoughts and heartaches with our recitations and remembrances of Amitābha and the Pure Land. The Buddha-name can be a refuge from thoughts of self-harm, from self-criticism and cynicism when these thoughts come unbidden. In mental strife, we can bring Amitābha to mind as a break from the down-pressing emotions assailing us.

○
———

We do not have to be mindful while we recite or hold our mind in any particular way. Simply say the Buddha-name; that is enough. Reflecting on the Pure Land is another comfort of the Pure Land Way. We can follow the descriptions in the Contemplation Sutra or reflect on our own, in our own way. With our imaginative eye we can take a look around the Pure Land and see places that inspire the heart. Although we would all love to have visionary experiences of the Pure Land, this is not necessary or common. The simple act of bringing your mind back to the Buddha-name or to a feature of the Pure Land makes the connection with Amitābha.

Initially, we need to put in a little effort to pick up the Buddha-name habit. Start off saying or thinking it every time you have a very pleasant experience, such as when you taste something delicious or when you feel the blankets get delightfully warm on a cool evening.

After a few days of that, add in saying or thinking the Buddha-name every time something happens that is unpleasant, such as stubbing your toe or hearing about something sad happening. We are acclimating ourselves and our recitation of the Buddha-name to not be limited to the good or to when we are in the mood to recite.

Amitābha's name can accompany us into the disturbing parts of our lives as well. There is nothing which can stain or defile Amitābha, there is nothing which needs to be hidden from Amitābha. We are who we are and Amitābha loves us. So, in our anxiety and worry, bring him in; in our rage, bring him in; in our jealousies, bring him in. There is both a stillness and a vibrancy to Amitābha when we hold him in our heart. He is like a quiet meadow in the morning, and he

O

_____

also holds an intensity of spiritual light as if he were a sun roiling with a mix of wisdom and compassion.

Some find counting recitations to be useful in starting to recite Amitābha's name. One way to do this is to calculate how many recitations we make in one minute. It is easier for us to track how many minutes we spent reciting while we are out and about in our day than it is to keep track of what number we are on when counting each recitation as we go along. For example: I recited for about ten minutes on the drive to work, three minutes at the elevator, and two minutes while on hold on a telephone call, for a total of fifteen minutes this morning. Now in one minute I recite fifty times, so fifteen times fifty is 750 recitations. It should not be too hard to reach 10,000 a day. Once you find your mind regularly returning to the Buddha-name you can stop counting and making much effort. The goal is for the Buddha-name, and thereby Amitābha, to be a continuing presence in our daily life.

What is most important is the heart connection to Amitābha and the Pure Land. The deeper our inspiration, the more we just naturally recite the Buddha-name. So use the arts to inspire you. Find images that take your breath away: photographs, prints, sculptures. Look at paintings, both antique representations of Amitābha and contemporary expressions. The arts provide us an access to Amitābha through our imaginal faculty; we feel a sense of kinship with him through his image. The joy of connecting to Amitābha at this level has brought on a flourishing of the arts in every culture into which the Pure Land teachings have spread widely.

Keeping up inspiration will be important in maintaining the Buddha-name habit. Many wear a string of beads on their wrist or they

○
————

wear jewelry with the gemstones of the types found in the Pure Land as a reminder to recite the Buddha-name and as a way to touch back to their inspiration and faith in the midst of their busy day.

Finally, should you lose your inspiration and stop reciting the Buddha-name for a while, do not feel guilty. Amitābha does not get angry, so there is no need for you to feel bad. Simply start back up saying the Buddha-name.

○
————

Carried by the Buddha-Name

The Buddha-name carries me on its back
Over treacherous streams
Of evil thoughts.
Rock to rock,
Boulder to boulder,
We pass over
my hateful tendencies
Toward discord and anger.
We step around the spiteful words that cut to the core
And we jump right up and over my self-righteous indignations
To land on the other bank,
Sukhāvatī itself.
I sit down in the fine waterside grass
So that I can rest from all my human trials and travails.
The dharma winds gently blow
And the flower blossoms
Bob and nod with understanding.
I lie back to bask
In Amitābha's golden glow.

○
———

A Man Broken on the Wheel of Life

He was a bare-fisted barroom brawler
And I got to know him at his end.
A curved over husk of who he had been,
His spirit hadn't faded a bit.

Now he just couldn't quite believe
In Amitābha's golden light,
But he knew his own karma
Was dark and thick like tar.

He was gentle on the inside
In a world that had always
Handled him harshly.

Now that he is gone,
I dedicate my Buddha-name recitations
To him, tonight,
Hoping that he will be carried forward toward the Pure Land
And not be trapped in further lives to be painfully lived.

I want the pit bull bite of karma to let him go
To stop shaking him
And let him find the peace
He has yet to know,
For I never saw a man

○
───────

Struggle more
Just to smile.

So I call to Amitābha earnestly
For this man.

Oh how I hope that when I get to the Pure Land
He is waiting to greet me,
To tell me of his agonies and his reprieve
And his great relief
In the release
From all that drove him to anger.

Please, Amitābha, please.

Lotus Birth

○
———

It's Too Simple to Believe

Many spiritual seekers associate Buddhism with intricate meditation and visualization practices. To now come across the practice of Buddha-name recitation, which is so simple, is almost too much to believe. Yet they should reflect: Wouldn't a Great Buddha, who is even praised by other Buddhas, find a way to create a simple path to enlightenment for us foolish and traumatized human beings? Amitābha sees how difficult it is for us in this realm of life, so he has made an alternate state of being for us to go to after death, rather than our being poured back into the viciously churning human world for another life.

In his Pure Land we can engage with the truths of reality with the full support of a loving community. There, we do not struggle for enlightenment on our own, but are part of a people who are all moving steadily toward enlightenment.

Just saying the Buddha-name regularly and placing our hearts on rebirth in the Pure Land is enough for us to find ourselves in the Pure Land in our next life. We do not have to focus our mind to a fine point; our actions do not have to be perfectly pure; Amitābha knows we are confused and still he helps us. This help is everything. We are protected by Amitābha in this life, and he pulls us out of the endless chain of painful lives with the sureness of a firefighter taking hold of us in a burning building. So this practice of reciting Amitābha's name appears simple, but it is the basis of a deep connection to Amitābha that will see our sufferings end in his Pure Land.

Amitābha on the Mind

Just having our minds on Amitābha
Keeps our minds from tangling themselves
In a thicket of confusions.
Our greedy lusts bind and twist us
Into a matted mess
Like the hair that gathers
In a bachelor's shower drain.

Now as for our hatreds,
Their smoke chokes us
And traps us
In a constant, aggressive haze.

So think of Amitābha
And bathe your mind
In his loving light.
In doing this, you are occupying your thoughts
With something of reality,
Something of the essence of enlightenment.

○
___

Amitābha Is Closer Than the Pain

There is a barren place in my mind
All covered in soot
With hard-packed earth,
As it is the spot where I land
Again and again
Every time I am overwhelmed
In distress or depression.
Dropped down to where the desolation winds
Blow the flecks of soot off of the end of my nose,
All I can do is wrap myself around my woes
In hopes of some comfort I'd lost or let loose.

In the pressure cooker of anxiety,
I need a power greater than my own
To help me, to anchor me,
For my emotions tingle the death tingle.
Breath labored,
Mind circuitry
Flooded,
Decisions impossible,
More stress fatal?

I must call on reserves
Beyond my own
And some flight of fancy

Just will not do.
So I put all my trust
In Shakyamuni, the lion of the dharma.

He preached about Amitābha,
Described his vows in depth, and
Assured us that Amitābha could help us
After he was gone.

Shakyamuni also told us that
Every time we say Amitābha's name
He becomes aware of us.

So we can speak directly to Amitābha
About what we are going through,
What we are experiencing.
Amitābha understands,
For he has seen all of human pain.

In response, he has imbued his name
With spiritual power
So that even in our suffering
We can be close to him.

○
―――――

Shining on Me

If you could see
Amitābha's rays of light shining on me
As I recite his name,
I would appear to be but a blurry silhouette,
The same as a lone oak tree on a hill
When the sunset sun drops behind it.
You see a few branches
And a bit of the trunk,
But the rest
Is all kaleidoscopes
And light beams
Of orange-reds.

But the sun, it sets,
Amitābha's love light
Shines on through the darkest of times.

○
———

Woman in Front of Her Amitābha Shrine

○
_____

Twelve Reassurances

Whether practicing within one of the Pure Land traditions or individually relying on Amitābha, we share a similar heart resonance with this Buddha of infinite light and with each other. It is this heart resonance with Amitābha which can help carry us through unexpected trials and heartache. The inspiration which moves us can protect our hearts and minds, for we can turn our thoughts to Amitābha and the Pure Land for even the briefest of breaks from the onslaught of worry and anxiety. We can also say his name to soothe ourselves and others. Though an experience may be terrible, it is impermanent and will soon pass. It is but a small part of our experiences in the countless lives we have lived. Over and over we have suffered infirmity, helplessness, agony, and deaths, deaths, deaths. Now Amitābha is putting that process to rest for us. These are the sufferings of a final human life. Our next birth will be into the Pure Land.

1 I have placed my heart on rebirth in the Pure Land and I recite Amitābha's name. That is enough for me to be swept up in Amitābha's karmic momentum and be drawn along toward the Pure Land.

2 Amitābha Buddha's essence is a pure love. This love comes to me each time I recite Amitābha's name.

3 I do not have to fear being who I am, because Amitābha accepts me thoroughly. All my foolishness and warped ego actions can't dim the light of Amitābha's love coming to me. I

will suffer in this life from the results of my bad intentions, but Amitābha is a steady positive influence on me, the sun shining though the day may be cold.

4 My fellow Buddha-name reciters are my siblings, for it won't be long before we are all kin in the Pure Land.

5 When death finally comes I will not be alone, for Amitābha will be there to bring me back to the Pure Land. The beings of the Pure Land will rejoice at meeting me. I will be welcomed as a long lost relation.

6 My recitations of Amitābha's name are powerful karma. Should I fall into a coma or suffer dementia, it would not derail the momentum which is bringing me to the Pure Land.

7 My relationship with Amitābha is the only one which follows me through life, death, and rebirth. It is my most intimate relationship, Amitābha only a whisper, a thought away.

8 As in a vast net, I have been scooped up in Amitābha's love and care. He is protecting me in ways I cannot perceive or understand.

9 Following the Pure Land Way, I have broken the cycle of being reborn again and again into this human world full of dissatisfaction and disappointment. In the human realm I have plenty of greed, hatred, and delusion; and from these three, suffering inevitably follows. In the Pure Land, I will be illuminated in Amitābha's light of wisdom, my heart full of bliss, love, and compassion.

10 Reciting Amitābha's name is a last minute lifeboat available to all people as they go down into death. Even those who have

___O___

not believed their entire lives can, in the last moment, call to
Amitābha, and he will come to them.

11 My recitations can benefit those who have passed away.
Through dedicating my recitations to those who have recently
died, Amitābha can bring them to the Pure Land.

12 Knowing that my life's road ends in the Pure Land changes the
journey. Many possibilities for selfless action open up.

Immutable

Amitābha gives us ground to stand on
In a shifting world where nothing lasts.
We bring him to mind again and again
Amidst all of these fears of frailty in this life,
Our final end
Ever threatening.
Even in downtrodden times,
We can pour Amitābha into our minds
And let those hurtful thoughts float away
Like drowned flies,
Their little corpses spinning and spinning
Away,
Away,
Away.

Amitābha Responds (to Addiction)

○
──────

On the Run

On the run from what I have done,
The hounds of karma
Are close behind me.
In hopes of losing the scent
Of all my bad deeds of body, speech, and mind,
I race down to the river of my spiritual energy.
But I find the river low,
More a series of pools
Than any kind of flow of transcendent higher consciousness.

The barking gets louder
And I hurry on down the riverbed,
Scrambling over boulders of doubt
And thick clusters of rocky troubles.
Despite all of my exertions,
I become mud-stuck
In this groggy mess of confusion.
I cry out for some relief:
Amitābha, help me!

Whether due to my own good karma ripening
Or the grace of a Bodhisattva passing by,
Amitābha has entered my life.
He has come in low from upstream,
A frothing wave rushing around my ankles,

The swirling waters quickly freeing my feet
and tossing aside my karmic hounds.

Amitābha fills in the riverbed for me
With his resolve to save those who recite his name.
The buoyancy of the Buddha-name
Lifts me up into the current
Of the now flowing river.
Bobbing comfortably,
All the many pebbles of resentments I have collected in my pockets
Fall now to the river bottom.

No longer weighted down,
My spirit becomes light,
And I can stretch out my body as I float
And wiggle my toes downstream
Toward the Pure Land.

I still get scrapes and bangs and bounce off from
Submerged branches,
But at times it also feels like I am
Soaring in the Buddha-name
As I round another curve.

Now, when the white seabirds appear overhead
I'll know the ocean of bliss lies just ahead.
Time to leave this muddy river

For the clear waters of the sea
Where in the west
The sun hangs like a drum
Over the horizon.
Amitābha.

○
_____

On Waking

On waking, her mind fills with thoughts aching with criticisms.
Some come from deep inside her,
But most have the timbre of parents, friends, and enemies.
You can't . . . You won't . . . What if? . . . What then? . . . Unloved.
Rising from the pillow,
She sits up, casually cross-legged,
And shakes her head at all those thoughts.
Though they are too strong for her to fight,
She looks confidently to the little Amitābha photo on her bookshelf,
For he is all that is kind and true.
Bringing hands together in gassho, she bows.
"Oh, Amitābha, save me from these hateful intruders of my mind,
Clear away these inner critics."
She begins reciting Amitābha's name,
Awkwardly at first, in a sleepy voice that then clears.
Each Buddha-name proceeding from her lips
Moves like a plume of breath
Exhaled into a freezing winter's night.

Amitābha picks up her voice
While scanning the cosmos for those calling his name,
He hears her heart's cry.
His loving light shines in a flash toward her,
Covering her gently,
Like a down comforter tossed over a bed.

○
———

She reflects on Amitābha's total acceptance of her, his love for her,
Exactly as she is right now.
The bliss rises warm, thrilling her heart.

Help on the Way

○
───────

We Are Here Afloat

We have been thrown unceremoniously
Into the sea of human existence.
Adrift now for a very long time,
We are here afloat
In the far reaches
Of what people call normal.

Some of us are drenched in addiction,
Others tossed about by swells of bitter mental health,
And sadly, so sadly,
Many are drowning in loss and grief.

Oh Amitābha, send your light upon us!
Let us call your name in clear tones
Or gravelly voices.
Your name, your name
Said between coughs and cussing.

Bring us some small bit of the Pure Land now,
For our own bad karma has us by the throat.
Dreams and aspirations have become soggy
And sunk away.

Despite what we have done, Amitābha,
Despite what has happened to us,
Still you come

O
———

To save all
Who call
Your name.

Appearing warm on the horizon,
You cross this sea quickly
And pull up alongside us in your lotus boat.
The golden luster of your robes
Reflects from the giant white lotus petals.

For those of us here adrift,
You lower one of the petals into the water
So we may swim into its scoop
And be drawn back up onto the deck.
There, the lotus hull gives off a rich scent
Permeating the lush robes
Wrapped around us.

You welcome us, Amitābha, with a joyful smile.
Your light falls upon us.
Our hands,
Our faces
All begin to bear the golden radiance
That marks a member of your family.

It has been a rough journey, but we are safe at last,
Sailing with Amitābha back to the Pure Land.

○
———

A Last Hope Buddha

These Pure Land teachings
Are for the trapped,
The hemmed in,
The hammered down.

You see, Amitābha is a last hope Buddha,
One you can turn to in an instant
When everything else fails.

When every comfort, every closeness
Is far away,
Amitābha.

When greed spins out of control,
Amitābha.

When desires flame can't be put out,
Amitābha.

When there is no good option,
Amitābha.

With the sure pull of a siphon,
Amitābha will draw us to the Pure Land when our lives
Come to their end.

○
————

For now, we must endure what we must endure,
But our destination is clear, a new life in the Pure Land,
With enlightenment assured by Amitābha.
So we live with his radiance bright in our hearts
And find ways to enjoy the journey
Through this trying world
And on to the Pure Land.

○
_____

That Thing That Happened to Me

The terrible, unspeakable
That I went through
Has been a glut of phlegm
Choking me down,
But now I breathe clear in the light of Amitābha.
Each time I recite his name
I move forward a little more
Toward the bliss of Buddhahood,
And I move a little farther away
From the shitty happenings that stained me through.
Amitābha
Amitābha
Amitābha
Amitābha
Amitābha
Amitābha

○
———

Queen Vaidehi

We start in a dark place, as most spiritual journeys do. We see a queen in despair for her king. He lies starving in the dungeon placed there by her very own son, Prince Ajatashatru. She has been keeping King Bimbisara alive by sneaking food into him on her daily visits. Each morning her handmaidens mix honey and ghee into a paste that, along with grape juice, they hide inside her jewelry. Unfortunately, her son has found her out and storms into her chambers in such a rage that he draws his sword to kill her. However, the prince's ministers stop him, pointing out that it would be an abomination for a ruler to kill his own mother.

Pushed far beyond her limits, this powerful woman feels helpless in her grief. She is shell-shocked by the hurt, so deep and personal. Having learned that the Buddha is teaching on Vulture's Peak, not far away, she cries out for him. Through his psychic powers the Buddha hears her and projects himself into the cell where she has been imprisoned.

She pleads with him to show her some place where pain, such as she is experiencing, does not exist. The Buddha shows her all the many Buddhas and their Pure Lands throughout the cosmos. He points out Amitābha and his Pure Land, whose light shines the farthest and is the most wonderful.

Marveling at the tranquility of Sukhāvatī, Queen Vaidehi places her heart on taking birth there. In Sukhāvatī the spiritual conditions are

○
————

so perfect for growth that one moves quickly to an enlightened state of being. Queen Vaidehi is to become a Buddha.

Out of her deep empathy, she worries for all of the other people in the world and those yet to be born, for they would not be shown a vision of the Pure Land as she just had been. She asks the Buddha how these people will be inspired to go to Sukhāvatī. This is when Shakyamuni reveals, for all generations, the reflections on Amitābha, his Pure Land, and his vows in what we know as the Contemplation Sutra.

We can see in Queen Vaidehi our own despair and sense of overwhelm in times of crisis. In our suffering, at our most raw, there is an opportunity to open up to something greater than ourselves. Curled up in a fetal ball, a mind thick with distress, we can become willing to open our hearts to a power beyond ourselves. We can put our trust in Amitābha, accept the help he is offering and call out to him as Queen Vaidehi hoped we would.

In upheaval and anxiety, we can become crippled in nasty thought loops. Trying to be rational with ourselves in that type of situation seldom calms us. We need a wider perspective, we need support, we need love. We can tune ourselves back into Amitābha's love for us by reciting his name. No matter how bad things are in the moment, our true trajectory is bringing us into the comforts and delights of the Pure Land. There the troubles that plague us now will seem insignificant and are certainly nothing which could possibly hold back the wisdom waiting to enlighten us when we arrive in the Pure Land. This is the putting down of such troubles, forever. If we can just mud-

○
———

dle through these dilemmas and discomforts, a vastness of spirit will open within our hearts when we get to the Pure Land.

Now, we may cry out in our pain and frustration about how terrible this world is, and Amitābha would agree with us. This human realm is filled with all kinds of deceits and confusions, it is very, very difficult to make significant spiritual progress here. Even if we live a moderately ethical life, we are still destined to head back into another human body for the same kind of pain as we are experiencing now. Amitābha wants to help us avoid all of that suffering and gnashing of heart. This is why his invitation to the Pure Land is so precious; it is our chance to escape countless agonies.

Through Queen Vaidehi's pain we are liberated, for she has pointed us in the direction of Amitābha. In his light our ultimate fate is settled. No longer are we at the mercy of our rebirth and our karma; a stronger force exerts its power over us. Amitābha is leading us toward our enlightenment. We are loved and part of the sangha of the Pure Land. We are in Amitābha's family, and Queen Vaidehi is our great hero.

Queen Vaidehi Calling Shakyamuni Buddha

○
———

Peaceful Fool

I am happy to be just a peaceful fool.
I have given up on knowing grand wisdoms,
And I am content with the simplest of Buddhist practices:
The saying of Amitābha's name.

I laugh at myself
When the silly selfish thoughts come fast and thick.
What did I just think about that person?
Where did that come from?
Well, my shadow karma has deep roots within me,
And I have dug as deep as I can go, trying to remove them.
But still they remain.
However, Amitābha can free me from what has me stuck,
He can ensure
That in my next life I will not be gripped
by the mayhem in my mind,
For he will take me to his Pure Land,
Where all bad intentions whither in the refined atmosphere
Of Sukhāvatī.

For now, all I can do is say the Buddha-name again,
And chuckle a fool's chuckle
At all the thoughts that my bad karma produces in my mind.

Under the Trees

○
———

Amitābha Is Not Afraid of Me

I know what people think of me,
But a dog that's been kicked around
Looks mean, too.
Thankfully, Amitābha Buddha
Takes me as I am
And I will be taken to the Pure Land.
I'll go right alongside others more wholesome than myself,
For Amitābha loves us all equally.
Anyone can whisper Amitābha's name.
It's so simple,
Yet, it has so much power.

O
___

My Image of Myself

Somewhere deep down in the gullet of my beliefs
I don't think I am worthy of enlightenment.
Despite my good works and kindnesses,
My nasty ways and selfishness
Cast a shadow over my image of myself.

To my great relief,
This doesn't prevent Amitābha from loving me
And accepting me exactly as I am.
He cradles me gently, a baby bird fallen and found.

Death of a Reciter (Swirling Bodhisattvas)

○
_____

Expeditious Buddhism

Many choose the Pure Land Way because it is their quickest path to becoming a Buddha. They know that if they were to attempt to gain enlightenment by their own efforts that it would take lifetimes to achieve. With Amitābha's help, they can look forward to becoming a Buddha in their next life in the Pure Land.

Living another human life in this world is a frightening prospect: the wrenching teenage years, the losses of loved ones, the aches of old age. All this awaits us if we don't arrange for our escape in this current life.

Often, fear of death is a motivator for those taking up the Pure Land Way. Knowing that they will be met in the moment of death by Amitābha, they feel a sense of relief, in that they will escape the spirit-crushing ordeal of the intermediate state between our death and our next birth. Instead, they will quickly be born into Sukhāvatī.

Some take up reciting the Buddha-name because they strive to be able to truly help others on a deep and profound level. They want to become a Buddha as quickly as possible so that they can return and rescue more people from this world.

To Enlightenment

In the peril of this world
I am not strong enough to swim
To the far shore . . . through meditation.
My efforts have been a mere thrashing around,
Making little headway.
Thankfully, I am rescued through the Buddha-name.
I grasp hold of it and see that I can float
And wait
For Amitābha
To approach.

Reunion in the Pure Land

○
_____

The Sweet Name

Amitābha gave us his name
As a mother gives her child a sweet candy
While standing in line at the bank.

Our mind and mouth can say and savor the Buddha-name.
It distracts us from succumbing to our fussing and foolishness.

○
_____

Trampled On

She was a trampled-on young woman,
Life had already walked hard upon her.
That anxious brow
Told of how
Everything was a struggle.

Yet going out the door,
No matter how late she might already be,
She never missed making three quick bows
To a plastic Amitābha on her little shrine.

Her recitations of the Buddha-name
Slowly polished the
Tiny crystals and gems
She had laid out in a sliver of a moon arc.

"Amitābha is all I really have,"
She said once
During a back porch break
From the crowded revelries which were going on inside.
"And you know, I think that is enough."
I agreed, so we promised to meet up with each other
In the Pure Land,
And she is over there now.

○
———

The first thing she said she was going to do
Was to wade into one of the pools lined with gold dust sand
Just so she could feel gold squishing between her toes.

Me? I just want to
Fly, fly, fly like I have in a dream.

It will be so good to catch up with her,
And she can show me around the Pure Land
With her toes all sparkling gold.

Now this is no eulogy,
Just a voicing of rejoicing
That a person, tumbling through life,
Can call the Buddha-name
And find equilibrium
In Amitābha's light.

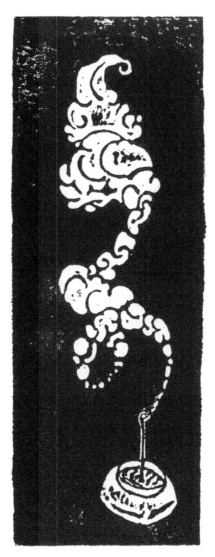

Incense Offering

○
———

For the Santa Cruz Mountains

Oh, it is so good to be back on
The spine of my spiritual mountain range.
The great number of times I have wound up and up
These mountain roads
In search of my enlightenment,
In zendo, Tibetan temple, or solitary cabin,
Going up the mountain to go down deep.

Over the years, I have driven up so many carloads of people
bound for retreat and a trip of self-discovery.
They often had that slight excited fear of the unknown
or an uneasiness as to what they might learn about themselves.
Yet on the way home, it was clear
A bond had been made with the Buddha.

On this journey, I came alone,
The winding turns pressing only me side to side in my seat.
When night finally comes to the forest,
I enter the realm of just being.
I shed all that was important yesterday
And secure my future in the Pure Land
With just the Buddha-name.
I come to offer praise,
To make my solitary salutation
And to spend more time with you, Amitābha.

○
_____

The Types of Things People Say to Amitābha

Amitābha is our close parent, both mother and father. We can speak to them directly in a personal tone of conversation. Amitābha is confidante, friend, protector.

"You are my Buddha, Amitābha."

"Hey, Amitābha, Amitābha, Amitābha it's me again."

"Protect me, Amitābha, protect me."

"Amitābha, I am really hurting today."

"Oh, Amitābha, the suffering of this world!"

"It is a beautiful day, Amitābha, I offer you this bliss."

"Amitābha, I am yours and your love is mine."

Amitābha Arrives

○
_____

49 Days

(Referencing the *Bardo Thodol*, a.k.a. *Tibetan Book of the Dead*)

Before coming into this life,
Even before the interaction of
Egg, sperm, and my consciousness,
I spent forty-nine days
In the in-between state, the bardo between
My previous death . . . and the conception that led to this life.

From the moment
I burst free from my last body,
The confusion and desperation began.
Blown forward with the incredible force of my karma,
I was completely helpless in directing my destiny.
A disorientation set in,
With periods of swooning . . . and coming back aware again.
I was flowing loose amongst countless beings breaking down
And taking form again.
It was simply terrifying to my unenlightened consciousness.

I was in a panic, looking for a familiar perch
So I quickly nudged myself between another set of parents,
My parents.

○
─────

Here in this life I am living, now,
I have temporarily escaped the swirling maelstrom
Of the in-between state.

Thanks to Amitābha,
This time, as I approach my end,
I will be freed in the moment of death.
I will not come back around to a baby's babble,
For Amitābha is already secreted away within me.
Soon I will be broken out of the cycle of my delusions.
I wait, with the patience of a prisoner
Listening for the sound
Of a familiar car engine
On the other side of the wall.

When I do step into my death,
Amitābha will come for me with a crowd of bodhisattvas
All playing their stunning music
As they descend from rainbow clouds.
I will swoon again,
But this time because I am overwhelmed with joy.

Then I will find myself in the Pure Land,
Inside a giant lotus bloom bulging pregnant with me.
I'll feel the gentle, slight sway of the lotus stalk beneath me,
Hear the little splashings of the vast shimmering pool
In which it grows.

○
———

The lotus bloom will open,
The petals gently parting above my head
And I will be lit up with Amitābha's radiance
Starting from the top of my head, down my shoulders
To my torso and, finally, my folded legs.
With my lotus fully open,
I will be illuminated in ecstatic light
And I will stretch a good sleep's stretch,
Amazed at how rejuvenated I feel.
Then I will look to Amitābha
And bow with all my being.

While Waiting to Go to the Pure Land

Days following days,
Just trying to get by.
Yet we have already fulfilled a life's pure purpose
By connecting with Amitābha.

Living out this life,
We are fortunate to have the Buddha-name
To carry us,
A wonderful carriage pulled by powerful syllables
Which ensures that we are destined for the Pure Land.
The passing views
Show us the true impermanence of what we experience in this life.
Trying times, nasty people,
Are all just rolling by
With the landscape through which we travel.
So we live in the insecurity of this world
With Amitābha's name on our lips.

Souvenir from a Dream: With New Friends in the Pure Land

○
_____

I Say the Buddha-Name

I say the Buddha-name
When my own mind tries to hurt me.
That bitchy, critical voice turning its vitriol on me,
Saying I'm this,
Saying I'm like that.
No.
I choose to fill my mind with Amitābha.
I'll say his name
I'll think of him
Every time the hurtful chorus
Starts to put poison in my ear.

So come at me again, my inner critic.
I know you can't resist,
But you will have to cross
The vast moat in my mind: Amitābha's name.
It spreads out before me
And circles all the way around me.
His name is deeper than you think it is,
Thousands of fathoms
Of wisdom, kindness, and love.

In Case of Spirits

Spirits!
Now that you are here,
Come into the circle of Amitābha's light,
Which is already shining down upon me.
Tuck yourself into his light
As if an overhang used to avoid a downpour,
The cloudburst of all your despair.

As I say the Buddha-name,
You will come to know Amitābha
In the waves of my voice.
Let me speak the sounds
That you are unable to make for yourself
So that you, too,
May find yourself embraced by Amitābha
And born into the Pure Land.

◯

Inspired by Enlightenment

With hearts inspired by enlightenment, we want to break free of our suffering, but our time left in this life is too short to follow Shakyamuni's example of intensive meditation practices. Therefore, when we die, we face being born into another human life, into conditions beyond our control. While we hope to continue our practice of the Buddha's teachings, who knows if they will cross our path in the next life? Will we have the time and dedication to gain enlightenment in that life before we die, yet again?

This is why finding the Pure Land Way is such an incredible opportunity. Instead of risking the pains of another human life in the attempt at enlightenment, we can be born into the Pure Land where our enlightenment easily happens. Our inspired hearts have Amitābha's assurance that they will become the hearts of Buddhas.

She Will Go to the Pure Land

○
——————

Treasure the Buddha-Name

As snowshoes across a snowed in landscape
The Buddha-name
Keeps us from getting stuck
In the cycle of human births.
It delivers us to our enlightenment.
So treasure the Buddha-name,
For it has rescued us when all was lost.

___○___

Sunset

This evening little swirls of fog
Catch rainbow light
Before the setting sun,
While Amitābha's light
Shines on all reciters of his name.

They all glow alive
For but a brief moment.

○
─────

When I Descend

When I descend into the great hollow of my dying
And no longer remember my own name,
Amitābha will appear with a long retinue
Come to welcome me to the Pure Land.

So Death, keep your threats and your fears,
Because you only have one more swipe at me.
Yeah, yeah, you will flip the switch as you always do,
Lights out whenever you choose,
But rather than the usual death terrors you bring,
Instead of that,
My lotus will be opening in the Pure Land,
And I will be with Amitābha.

Bullies Waiting

○
___

Something Sweet

Ah, this bliss,
This bliss I offer to you, Amitābha.
What I love, I share with you,
For I am so very grateful that you are helping me.
Before long, you will guide me into Sukhāvatī.
Oh, the joyful reveries
As you bring my mind into clarity.
With your help, I will shed the harmful and become one of the wise.
Opening my heart into the full blossom of Buddhahood
Will truly be the sweetest thing of all.

Community and Sangha in the Pure Land Way

With few Pure Land temples and sanghas outside of Asia, Buddha-name reciters elsewhere can look to the example of the early Pure Land associations, which met in small groups to discuss the Pure Land perspective on life and to recite the Buddha-name together. We will see what kinds of communities and pods of practitioners form in coming years, as the Pure Land Way continues to inspire more people.

Meanwhile, we can connect online with the existing Pure Land traditions, which are large in other parts of the world, or we can make friendships and form something new for ourselves. The Pure Land Way is appropriate for isolated Buddhists far from others, as the connection with Amitābha is a direct one and does not require an intermediary or a dedicated place of worship. We simply say the Buddha-name.

When we take up reciting the Buddha-name, we become part of the sangha of Sukhāvatī. They are all cheering us on, wishing us well and looking forward to welcoming us to the Pure Land when the time comes.

Trees in Pure Land

Companion

Whether sung below a mountain peak
Or whispered back in my cubicle,
The Buddha-name is a fine companion.
I say it out to the Pure Land
Throughout my day.
Amitābha on my lips,
Amitābha in the Pure Land.

○
___

Turning toward Amitābha

Our life lights up as we turn toward Amitābha.
The grinding old bitternesses of arguments we lost long ago
Begin to melt away
As we reorient our lives toward our future life
In the Pure Land.
With a vaster perspective, large insults shrink into insignificance.
We truly live in the moment, aware that we are part of a continuum
Through our past lives into this one and then off to the Pure Land.
In this fleeting life, where do we wish to expend our energy?

Kūya in the Marketplace

○
———

Night Moth

Night moth, night moth
Flutter the dark window alone with me.
Flutter whoosh, flutter whoosh,
You find yourself between two me's
Each mirroring the other.

I find myself between
The bright heart me
And the dusky me,
Trying to choose my path
Every moment.
They are both laid out with karmic consequences.
Which way shall I go, little moth?
And can I go with wing-borne designs such as yours?

Dry evening winds tumble you, my tiny friend,
And I swear you are in ecstasy.
Bliss-filled wings
Sweeping and swirling
Shaking antennas
And moving ever toward the light.

If only my dedication
Were as strong as yours . . .
Oh, the possibilities!

Ah, but there is some light here for me tonight.
The moon is warm with tomorrow
And adds fire to my eyes
That I may see clearly
What the new day brings.

○
─────

Don't Be Sad for Me

When my karma has finally run thin
And my body is broken . . . and blue,
Don't be sad for me.
I have a lot to celebrate,
For I will be turned loose!
No longer tacked to the wheel
Of life after life.
The human habit
will be abandoned,
And I will be bound
For the Pure Land.

You see, Amitābha knows me,
Knows my voice
Calling his name.

When my breath has gone away
And it won't be coming back,
Amitābha will be there to meet me.
Oh, to be in that moment!
To finally be in his presence,
Just amazing!
His great golden radiance brighter than the sun
Yet, soft as the light from a lover's bedside lamp.

○
————

I will walk out the gates of old age, sickness, and death
And go with Amitābha back to the Pure Land.
There, I will step out onto my lotus, floating on a turquoise lake.
I'll take my seat and listen to teachings, directly from Amitābha,
Which free my heart and purify my mind.

So don't be sad for me,
And you have a bountiful life yourself!
When you finally do arrive in the Pure Land,
Come find me.
Look for the musicians up in the clouds floating above,
And I'll be down there below,
On top of one of the bridges
that curve over clear canals,
There, where everyone dances in bliss.
I suspect that is where I'll be spending a lot of my time.

Bridge over Canal

○

Inspirations

In the Pure Land Way, we face outward from this life. Although involved in the world, we are not completely worldly. We look forward to our coming life in the Pure Land, our enlightenment, and then all of the many people we will be able to help. Limited in this life, we can only do so much, so we hold a place for Amitābha in this world, his light rotating within our heart each time we say the Buddha-name.

W e have a comfortable relationship with Amitābha. We are not petitioning for help; we are not throwing ourselves down on the ground begging for mercy. Amitābha already loves us. We just say the Buddha-name and accept that we are loved so much that, when this life ends, we are to be enlightened with all of our pain taken away, never to return.

The Pure Land Way is a path of faith. One has a heart response to Amitābha Buddha, serene and wise. There is detected in Amitābha something deep that calls to the depths of heart within us.

○
———

My habitual selfishness muddies my mind, leaving it like an old, half-buried milk bottle; yet, through all of that grime Amitābha sees me as a vessel for enlightenment.

We have the opportunity right now, while we are conscious and aware, to make the choice to be born into the Pure Land. We may not get this chance again for many, many lives.

As for ethical practice, we are going to become Buddhas, so we should do our best, now, to act more like one. When we fail in our attempts, we do not lose the love of Amitābha. With our transgressions, we only embarrass ourselves in front of him. We learn humility in our failings and how much we need Amitābha's help if we are to ever see an end to our sufferings.

A man with a circle symbol above a short horizontal line.

Amitābha's light can melt our numbness.

Amitābha has vowed to accept and rescue those who are the worst amongst us. He is not vindictive and has no interest in punishing us. Punishments come naturally from the ripening of bad karma, prickly and impossible for us to avoid. Amitābha helps us to escape to enlightenment.

$\bigcirc$

As we think of Amitābha, we can see him as within our heart, over our head, or in front of us. All are worshipful ways to relate to Amitābha.

Y_{ou} can bring peace to your spirit in the midst of addiction. Relax into Amitābha's total acceptance of you. Say the Buddha-name.

Some of us have no other choice than the Pure Land Way. The religion of our birth has failed us. Of all spiritual paths, only Buddhism calls to our hearts, but we are unable to make the incredible effort necessary to gain our enlightenment. The blade of our mind is far too dull and nicked up to be sharpened into the extraordinary sword needed to cut through our delusions and open our way to enlightenment. As our last hope, we recite the Buddha-name. We depend upon Amitābha to lead us out of human ignorance and to shelter us in his Pure Land. There, he will help our enlightenment to open within us.

O
_____

Our devotional attitude is one of gratitude. We acknowledge that we do not always know what is the correct ethical or karmic action to take, that we are clueless as to the true nature of reality. This is why we are grateful for what Shakyamuni Buddha has taught and for Amitābha's direct help in guiding us to our enlightenment.

O
_____

Our small needs are quite petty from a Buddha's perspective. So we should not bother Amitābha with our every want and whim. If you just want an easy life, Amitābha does not provide that. He saves us from the great fears in the intermediate state between our death and next birth. He intervenes so that we do not have to live through the pains of human life again. He is the catalyst for our enlightenment. These are the wonderful things for which we are thankful to him. So don't make foolish requests of Amitābha and you won't be disappointed.

○
_____

By reciting the Buddha-name we tap into the goodness of Amitābha. People can become aware of that. They may sense a stillness, even a deep joy within us. A joy in savoring the meaning we've found in life, knowing that we are now destined toward the Pure Land and our enlightenment.

The Buddha-name is a safe harbor for our hearts.

O
———

Our hope lies with Amitābha and his tremendous spiritual powers developed through eons of meditation practice. Our own spiritual efforts, they squeak and squeal, rusty wheels on an old tricycle. Amitābha hums and vibrates with a smooth motorcycle idle spitting power and wonder. Although we pedal for all we're worth, we may never get up the speed we need to be freed from all of our pains and disappointments. However, Amitābha offers us a ride. If we trust in him, we can hop on and hold tight by reciting his name. He'll rev us through the backed up traffic of our delusions and power us out onto the open road, the freedom of the Pure Land.

The Buddha-name is our touchstone, revealing reality when the comings and goings of life confuse us.

○
———

Amitābha is our companion through this fleeting life. The Buddha-name is where we meet. There, we also join in with the great turning of Buddhas in the cosmos, working for the benefit of all beings.

Amitābha said that his name is, literally, him. So, say it frequently and spend time with Amitābha.

The only prerequisite is that your heart be inspired by Amitābha Buddha. Beyond that, the saying of the Buddha-name is all that is left to do.

O
──────

The Pure Land Way is a path of two Buddhas: first, Shakyamuni Buddha, the historical person who gained enlightenment and told us about Amitābha Buddha; then, Amitābha, the Buddha of infinite light and love, who is constantly searching for those who call his name.

Amitābha gives us hope for our future, the time when we can put down the human hassle. Buddhas, we will be Buddhas.

○

Pause, every once in a while, just pause in the Buddha-name.

In the Pure Land

○

Glossary

Amitābha The Buddha of infinite light who loves us exactly as we are and wants to help us to gain our enlightenment.

bardo An in-between state such as the state we enter after death and before we are conceived for our next birth. The dream state is a bardo, as is our waking life. Bardos are described in depth in the *Bardo Thodol*, a.k.a. *Tibetan Book of the Dead*.

bodhisattva A being of great compassion who puts off their own enlightenment to help others first.

Buddha One who has woken up to the truths of reality, who sees things as they truly are. Great Buddhas have awesome powers to help other beings, including the ability to create their own Pure Land, a place where beings can get aid in gaining their enlightenment.

Buddha-name The name "Amitābha" or one of its variations, such as Amida, which is recited in order to take rebirth in the Pure Land. Known as nembutsu in Japan and nien-fo in China.

dharma wheels Buddhist symbol in the shape of a wagon wheel said to appear on the bottoms of a Buddha's feet as one of the marks of enlightenment. The "turning of the wheel of the dharma" means to teach the Buddhist path.

enlightenment Said to be like putting down a heavy load that has been carried for a long time. The end of the sufferings we have known in human life. A state of bliss. Seeing the true nature of reality.

O
___

gassho Placing the palms of the hands together and bowing to the Buddha.

Hōnen Originally a Tendai Sect priest, he turned to the Pure Land Way after extensive study of the Buddha's teachings. His exile from Kyoto to Shikoku began the spread of the Pure Land teachings across the countryside and, eventually, around the world. Hōnen had a number of disciples who started Pure Land traditions or sects of their own, including Shinran, founder of the Jodo-Shinshu traditions.

karma The planting of seeds in our consciousness with our deeds and intentions, which later bear good or bad results for us in this life or in our future lives.

Kūya Known as the Hijiri or Holy Man of the Marketplace. He would ring a gong and recite the Buddha-name in public places. Kūya was also known for his social work and public works projects.

linocut print Similar to a woodcut, the linocut print is made by carving the reverse of the image you wish to print into a sheet of linoleum. Ink is then applied with a roller and the paper pressed down and lifted back up to show everywhere that was carved away as white, while what was not carved away picked up the ink and transferred it to the paper.

meditation Quiet exercises involving mindfulness or insight reflection for the purpose of developing oneself to the point of enlightenment.

moxa stick In Chinese herbal medicine an herb stick burned and held above an injured part of the body.

○

_____

nembutsu or nenbutsu Japanese for reciting the Buddha-name.

nien-fo In China, refers to reciting the Buddha-name.

path of meditation Also known as the path of sages, this refers to all of the schools of Buddhism that use self-power practices in their striving for enlightenment. This is as opposed to the Pure Land Way, which relies on the other power of Amitābha to bring us to our enlightenment.

Pure Land A place of spiritual refuge created by a Buddha through the great powers they have gained through eons of spiritual discipline and meditation. When we are born there, we still have spiritual work to do, but it is far easier to make progress in the excellent conditions of the Pure Land.

sangha A Buddhist community or fellowship. In the Pure Land Way, the sangha are considered to be all of the beings in the Pure Land right now as well as the fellow Buddha-name reciters here in this world.

Shakyamuni (Gautama Shakyamuni) The historical person who was the first to become a Buddha in our world. In his teachings, he mentions Amitābha over 200 times.

Shandao From China, his writings influenced Pure Land Buddha-name practice in Japan and now in the English-speaking world. At the time of this writing, there is very little of his work that has been translated into English. We must look to Hōnen, for now, to experience Shandao's thought.

Sukhāvatī The name of Amitābha's Pure Land.

○
———

Resources

Amida Order: www.amidashu.org
Jodo Shu: www.jodoshuna.org
Jodo-Shinshu: www.buddhistchurchesofamerica.org
Shandao Lineage: www.purelandbuddhism.org

O
_____

Suggested Reading

Traversing the Pure Land Path: A Lifetime of Encounters with Hōnen Shonin. Edited by Jonathan Watts and Yoshiharu Tomatsu. Jodo Shu Press, 2005.

The Three Pure Land Sutras: The Principle of Pure Land Buddhism. Edited by Jodo Shu Research Institute. Jodo Shu Press, 2014.

The Three Pure Land Sutras. Translated by Hisao Inagaki. BDK America, 2006.

The Promise of Amida Buddha: Hōnen's Path to Bliss. Translated by Joji Atone and Yoko Hayashi. Wisdom Publications, 2011.

Plain Words Along the Pure Land Way. Translated by Dennis Hirota. Ryukoku University, 1989.

No Abode: The Record of Ippen. Dennis Hirota. University of Hawai'i Press, 1986.

Shapers of Japanese Buddhism. Yusen Kashiwahara and Koyu Sonoda. Kosei Publishing Co., 1994.

Naturalness, A Classic of Shin Buddhism. Kenryo Kanamatsu. World Wisdom, Inc., 2002.

Liturgy for Birth (Ojoraisan). Translated by Zuio H. Inagaki. 2009.

River of Fire, River of Water. Teitetsu Unno. Doubleday, 1998.

○
———

About the Author

John Del Bagno (JDB) is a poet, spoken word performer, self-taught visual artist, and gerontologist. He was ordained in the Triratna Buddhist Order for many years and was one of the founders of the San Francisco Buddhist Center. After meditating every day for over two decades, he turned to the Pure Land Way which relies on Amitābha Buddha and the recitation of the Buddha-name. JDB has journeyed to Japan to walk the ancient Buddhist pilgrimage routes in Kamakura, Shōdoshima, and Shikoku. In the USA he has made many retreats and lived alone for a year in a van in the National Forests of the Pacific Northwest, reciting the Buddha-name to the mountains, rivers, and highways.

JDB founded Pure Land Arts and the Gallery of Contemporary Pure Land Art to promote artistic communication of the Pure Land Way. He is the administrator of the Facebook group Inspiration for the Pure Land Way and hosts the YouTube channel Pure Land Poets.

purelandartwork.com

Printed in Great Britain
by Amazon

34188887R00088